INVISIBLE WINGS
The Power *of* Invisibility

DAWN CUMMINS

*Dedicated to Highly
Sensitive Souls,
who are blessing the
planet with their gifts.*

Thank you!

INVISIBLE WINGS

The Power *of* Invisibility

DAWN CUMMINS

INVISIBLE WINGS
The Power *of* Invisibility

First published in 2017 by
Panoma Press Ltd
48 St Vincent Drive, St Albans, Herts, AL1 5SJ UK

info@panomapress.com
www.panomapress.com

Cover design by Michael Inns
Artwork by Karen Gladwell

ISBN 978-1-784521-22-6

CONTENTS

ACKNOWLEDGEMENTS

Gratitude exudes from me,
I am filled with gratitude and love.

I am so grateful for the life I have chosen.

I am grateful to all my precious family,
what great teachers I chose!

I am still grateful to all my loved ones in heaven too,
they surround me always; you know who you are,
always encouraging me from afar.

Thank you all for helping me to feel whole,
achieving another goal.

All my blessings always,
from my Invisible Wings!

INTRODUCTION

Now is the time to really acknowledge yourself, and it is so necessary to realise that you are the Universe, Source, God, Divine Spirit. Embracing and owning your ability, understanding your knowledge of Invisibility, is very much a part of that understanding: it is powerful!

We are experiencing times that I would describe as a labour of love. To me, this feels earthy: communities are coming together, beginning to feel equal and more at peace with each other. I see this vision clearly and with love.

I believe we have an invisible support system, it is our inner guidance. The more you focus upon your inner divinity, the more Divine your life will become. Invisibility can certainly be the key to your transformation, supporting you, nurturing your self and your soul, knowing you will soon see positive results in your health and well-being.

Let your vulnerable side find its voice too, expressing only love, not fear.

Claim your thoughts of pure focus and intention as you go along your path to fulfil all your wishes; share how being a Sensitive Soul is rewarding in all aspects of your incredible life.

You have amazing intuition: feel "wowed" by it, trusting and knowing you have all your answers within.

Keep on believing in yourself: you are amazing!

The theme has to be love: it allows you to be invisible, as it is sustained when you are in it for the purpose of love. When you really love yourself, everything else in your life really works.

Love flows directly from source-god to you, and through you to others, for uplifting and healing. The unconditional love, the pure love that you naturally are, owns and becomes the most empowered soul so that you take back your power: you are in charge of your life.

You really are a true Earth Angel, and have been rewarded with your Angel Doctorate, an amazing revelation when receiving those Invisible Wings.

Dawn xx

PREFACE

The Power of Invisibility

I know and believe the power of Invisibility to be crucial regarding the well-being of Earth Angels, HSPs, (highly sensitive people, or carers on a mission to help others), empaths, introverts, and healers.

Invisibility is a powerful word, but equally an amazing gift. Really, it is our job to find a way for this sacred gift to take the lead, using this invisible thread of love and light.

The truth about Invisibility works in different ways, and I have learnt and now understand that there is more than one aspect of how invisibility can affect highly sensitive Earth Angels or healers. My own awareness and experiences led me to feel that not many people truly understand the depth of how Invisibility can be the key to maintaining health and well-being. Equally, I feel it is important that they also know the worthiness of being Invisible while in service, and embrace being recognised for their unique divine light. Learning to recognise themselves is equally important while doing the deep, divine, inner healing work they choose to do. The Universe really does want us to receive all the support that is available to us, to naturally let our light shine.

"Let there be light…"

- GENESIS 1:3
THE KING JAMES BIBLE

Then the outcome of your life's lessons does the inner work and works on your personal and spiritual development. These are both transformational and life-changing, helping you to become the Master of your own Destiny and defining self-mastery.

"In-visible" means to go in-side and be visible there, where you maintain visibility, allowing you to focus more on your internal life, peeling back the layers of your outer life. Acknowledge and embrace the connection to your inner self, your "god-self", bringing positive energy into every moment, where you will no longer require any outside attachments from the world.

They say that a true warrior requires nothing from the external world but to focus on peace at all times, helping to correct the outer chaos in the world, not feeling concerned with the outcome of the whole, but to continue connecting to their own deep, inner, peaceful world, from where peace and understanding will arise.

We are all pioneers in service, showing up, shining our light, as the world needs our divinity, not so much our humanity. Divinity does not necessarily require you to be holy as such, but more to express being spiritual and while at the same time human, trusting the divine spirit within and being open to all the amazing opportunities surrounding you right now. There is enough suffering and still the need for many sources of transformation.

We are born to take this power out into the world, experiencing it as the life-changing force that brings joy to many. It is a path that allows you to let go of attachments that do not serve you any more, through surrendering, releasing and letting go. You will start to experience more spiritual growth, be more in command of your loving powerful presence, knowing and feeling the pure love and what it truly means.

Practising the art of stillness, connecting to your presence, can be achieved from practising meditation and prayer. Prayer does not need to be tied to an organised religion; it is a spiritual tradition that many people have practised for hundreds of years, allowing them to truly connect to their presence and helping to surrender control and achieving grace.

Remember the power of prayer to help with every situation.

Grace is gratitude: remembering, asking, connecting, embracing the every day realities of our lives with thankfulness. Grace shows us ease and flow so that we can benefit from slowing down, gently receiving angel connections every day so that when we are in this flow of the divine source of grace, we also help others, reminding them too of the peace in the world that provides solutions or blessings of joy. Know that you can ask for the grace of the angels to work with you, and that you are always wrapped in their wings of pure love.

From sowing a tiny seed that grows inside and blossoms, comes clarity and inspiration. It shows you the way, providing miraculous change and blessings for all. An early sign that you are accomplishing this would be the experience of Invisibility, because then your invisibility would be for the purpose of love which is sustained as long as you are in it.

The power of invisibility is very much the opposite of what many people are striving for. The majority only seem to believe that the power of being visible is the answer, not realising that being Invisible is equally, if not more powerful. It's time to embrace and honour this new understanding and meaning of Invisibility, so start by accepting and allowing this power into your life. It is hugely empowering, especially when you know and become your own authority – this is your inner self, the authority of your life.

We can often spend much of our lives thinking others know better and looking outside of ourselves. But hopefully you will soon experience your "light bulb moment", proof of just how much you have stripped back those layers of doubt, transforming all negative thoughts about your abilities and desires to succeed, making your mind over, to then finding the answers to what you would do in situations as they arise. Truly beginning to trust and own your authority from within is a special moment of gratitude of your very own.

We are all unique individuals and we each have our place here in the world; we all choose to learn our lessons in our own way, and truly, there is no one like you. Some will be in service, out there and visibly supporting the whole, while others will choose to do deeper inner work, through being Invisible, but equally supporting the whole.

The world is focusing more and more on becoming visible, which makes overwhelm more apparent, especially, for example, for highly sensitive people, empaths, introverts who are wanting to grow in confidence. It is even more important to realise now that to be Invisible is such a strength, in fact a spiritual strength.

We all have a share in making a difference and helping the planet. This is the perfect time to share what goes on behind the scenes, expressing it through experience and example. This is all part of a preparation that will support our true life purpose.

Retreating more, accepting and honouring themselves, is so important; really thinking about taking more care of our energy, and knowing we have so much more to give. Trust that our actions will be divinely guided; this will help to transmute the causes of discord, removing the deep cores of fear, while being sustained by heaven's love.

Invisibility, as challenging as it can be, allows you to heal on a much deeper level, helping to stop the mind's addictive chatter and crazy pace and give up external stimulation, letting go and surrendering.

In time, when everyone else participates in this way, the changes created, which are not always visible, will also bring changes to the external world; it is about letting the Universe help us to change our direction. We leave all our old patterns behind, moving beyond all limitations to express freely and creatively, harmonising with mother Earth, bringing peace and abundance, as we continue to focus on our own deep inner powerful world.

The message is believing and knowing that the healing process is available for everyone who wants to shine their light and become a leader. But not everyone comprehends the message or understands the work of the world of Invisibility, and how collectively everyone makes a difference.

"I am a reflection on earth of the
Divine Spirit in Heaven"

My own healing experiences were challenged by others' misunderstandings, which is why I am so passionate about helping to support, encourage and inspire others about how Invisibility is there to help them. I want to show how other aspects of Invisibility are also about all the hard work that goes on behind the scenes.

Invisibility is fundamental in serving Earth Angels, light workers, sensitive souls, introverts and empaths, guiding them to take care of their well-being and health generally. Earth Angels, whether invisible or visible, are here to shine their light, share their gifts right here, right now, becoming as one.

"I spread my wings, I am an Earth Angel"

"Invisible Wings" of course, is what the book is called, and I am equally as passionate about Invisibility as I am about wings. When I think or talk about wings, I instantly think of angels and birds, especially the amazing condor. I was blessed to see one on a visit to Ecuador – what a privilege it was too. Eagles are also breathtaking; it is said that when the condor and eagle come together, it's a joining of one heart.

I think of the condor and automatically I close my eyes, opening my arms wide as I feel my heart expanding with love. This love in my heart gives me wings, helping me to soar towards my dreams, rising above any doubt or fear.

"May you have heaven in your heart, starlight
in your soul, and angels all around you."

I feel that wings represent wisdom, intuition, nature, gratitude, strength, all together equalling power. I love this quote:

"With brave wings, she flies."

I have deep feelings about this, it resonates, it really does come from being brave and bold, to experiencing a magical outcome.

"Until you spread your wings, you will have no
idea how far you can fly."

I really believe Angels live among us, and they hide their wings, but there is no disguising them, as you can feel the peace and hope they bring. You usually know how near they are when that feather appears, again you can feel their presence and the love they create in your heart.

> *"He will cover you with his feathers, He will*
> *shelter you with his wings. His faithful promises*
> *are your armour and protection."*
>
> – PSALM. 91.4

My Invisible journey has been so blessed, knowing the angels have been by my side as their wings of comfort have enfolded me with unconditional love.

The feeling really is more a "knowing", the conviction that you are really working on receiving your Angel Doctorate. They say to become an Angel, you need to act like one, which will make it easier to reach your accomplishments. Just like an Angel, you will experience being an objective witness, existing for the purpose of service, just like a form of higher education. Start by making yourself familiar with Angels, learning all you can, and find the deep joy in everything you do, just like the angels. Remember to pray for help, and simply feel the grace and ease of the angels as they offer you gentle assistance.

We all have a guardian angel from birth, keeping us safe, protecting, guiding, comforting, and constantly supporting us, unconditionally. They are beings of light who really do want to help us focus on our intentions, always encouraging us to ask for guidance, and receiving their love and healing. We are always surrounded by a team of loving angels, and when filled with faith, we are able to face situations with a much more positive outlook, trusting in the divine plan and infinite wisdom.

To the Angels, no job is too big or too small, they only ask for your thanks. Gratitude is knowing its importance and embracing it, especially when we are experiencing invisibility.

> *"One day I woke up in despair... a rising sun broke the darkness there... and on the horizon what did I see? A hundred of God's angels flying so high, my heart took wing, my eyes could see. The voice of my soul cried "I'm finally free", and then to my surprise, everybody flew to meet the angel band. The people of hate and the people of peace... all the opposites of the human race. The Mother and the Father too... the devils in me and the angels in you... and when the holy hour had come... in freedom we flew into the sun. We took no hate, we took no guns... the game was over, the battle done. Finally free, I'm finally free, I can fly like an angel."*
>
> *"Finally Free"*
>
> – DEBBIE SHAPIRO

Invisibility is transforming and it can be your instigator to feeling free, flying like an angel, surrendering, accepting, and allowing your deep powerful inner world to grow. Expanding, deepening as you fully experience the creator within, and helping so many others transform their own lives too. Allow the change and definitely keep on peeling back those layers, learn your many lessons by going within.

Let the change happen, becoming free of uncomfortable situations, letting it all go. Then when you start to relax, you will feel how exhilarating your energy is becoming, and how it is expanding into the new frequencies that are waiting to come into your presence.

Be open now, receive the divine light always, as it flows through and around you, as it grounds with the earth. You are a channel for spirit on Earth, rejoice in the transformation, as the world knows it to be.

Invisibility will lead you to the secrets of your spiritual voice; trust your higher self, as these secrets are ready to be discovered, you can now express your true life purpose. Listen with love to your inner voice, your life purpose is shining your inner divine light in ways that will bring you and so many others, joy and love.

Connect to your soul: this is your true identity. It is you, your true self. Use your voice to express your true essence, inspiring and influencing people. Let your voice lead, speak with love, showing compassion and connecting with others.

Magical qualities of synchronicity and freedom allow you to receive higher levels of expanded awareness, which benefit all of humanity. The new creation of a new life awakening is happening within and around you now.

The next nine chapters in this book will also help and support you to understand Invisibility from a level that can and will benefit you on your healing journey as an Earth Angel.

INVISIBLE

The Power *of* Invisibility

INVISIBLE

"Invisible you may be, learning how to be free… It may feel slow, 'cos only you will know, your inner strength and sincerity."

How does being Invisible affect you? Maybe you feel you would like to be more visible, perhaps.

Let us define the normal perspective of what invisible and visible mean. I am sure we all know the meaning, which is simply either to be seen, or not to be seen.

The world is changing and all for the better I feel; like all changes we cannot stop change – it happens anyway. Even words and their meanings seem to have certainly taken on a different trend too, and have a way of expressing some of those changes in a more positive way.

Changes are happening in more and more people. They are becoming more aware of personal development, helping themselves to train as life coaches, healers and helping others in many ways. There are so many in the world who are seeking help and needing support and encouragement to find their own inner strength, following and living their life purpose too, making their own difference in the world.

I totally support them and agree it is time to believe in ourselves, knowing we are good enough, and that we are doing enough, too. You are ready now to show your unique self, sharing your gifts, invisibly or visibly, either is absolutely fine.

I am passionate about this message of Invisibility, I want all Earth Angels to know they are so worthy of shining their light. Believe me, everything unfolds beautifully, and once on your path of self-mastery, you will soon discover what your life lessons are beginning to show you.

I am going to share an example of my own journey. It is still a work in progress, all about self-love and worthiness, a true lesson in finding myself, my true identity. I am very happy to have worked through many of my layers, I have remembered my truths, which are abundantly showing me the way forward.

Most of my life I had been a follower, while deep down I knew I could be the leader that I was born to be. For a good part of my life I chose to be a people-pleaser, wanting to be loved and liked. I was searching for that someone or something to help me feel valued and helping me to shine my light, but always thinking that an outside influence was the answer.

So many aspects of myself kept unfolding and still made me feel that I was meant to be visible. But, inside I knew I wasn't ready and honestly, at that stage, I didn't think I ever would be.

I continued to allow those same negative thoughts and strong feelings of feeling "lesser than", thinking that I wasn't achieving what others thought I should be achieving. Always feeling that I should be doing more. You know those niggling doubts, I'm sure you know the ones I am referring to: not believing in myself; my work was not as good as everyone else's and of course, they were much more professional than myself; my thoughts would have a really wonderful time.

But then I thought, "I don't do this... I should do that..." maybe it's time to start asking myself what *would* I do, if I trusted my intuition; after all I am my own inner teacher with all the best answers I could wish for.

Wow, it is massive when you start to realise that we are all wonderful beings of light, learning to believe in ourselves, understanding how special we truly are.

Love and worthiness issues, how we see ourselves, and healing from the inside takes huge courage. I decided to keep on embracing that courage that is inside myself, continuing to serve.

My transformation, my personal and spiritual growth was mind-blowing; it became life-changing as I began to feel this powerful and beautiful transformation in my heart.

I have felt very blessed knowing my life lessons would help others. The self-discipline I had and the motivation to want to help myself, believing that I could and would receive all the help I needed from the Universe, and being able to help others to help themselves, is so rewarding. Invisible or visible, if it is your soul's calling, choosing to do the inner work at some point on your journey, it will without question make huge differences along the way.

The term "peeling back your layers" that I seem to use quite a lot, means that at some point, you will truly understand and know the truth of being that sensitive soul. Those unfolding layers really do show that you are beginning to realise how Invisibility can be supportive when you start to embrace it, and then let it be the key to supporting your health.

The Universe eventually gets your attention through Invisibility, showing you how it can also be your protection. When you understand what happens when you begin to believe in yourself, you will know even more deeply the importance of how your experiences, (although they can still perhaps be challenging,) can and will improve your well-being, profoundly.

I will mention numerous times that it really does take courage to keep on digging a bit deeper. My personal biggest "light bulb moment" was when I woke up to the fact that my light was already shining, very brightly too, and realising it was ok and not always necessary to be visible in every situation.

I was working hard behind the scenes, doing my inner work, (as I like to refer to it), doing exactly what I was meant to do, going in-side and being in-visible there. Divine timing was, and still is, a huge part of the divine plan and is crucial for us all; we are all on our amazing journeys of the soul.

This is exactly why I feel the rest of the chapters of this book really will complement the power of Invisibility and support the resources we have available to us. My saviours were and are trust, faith, intuition (true knowing), belief and courage, with lots of divine love. My heart and soul guide me to be that messenger of love and prepare me, taking me out into the world, and becoming visible when my loving, powerful presence is needed.

The more you evolve, the more you will notice how much more sensitive you become to all the energies around you, hence being Invisible is your sacred transformational tool. So as a highly empathic and compassionate being, I draw on and use my spiritual tools to support my energy.

You will also realise how important it is that your nervous system has the chance to recharge, and it is paramount for you to use your spiritual tools (or gifts, if you prefer to refer to them in that way). It will all become more apparent as your role here on Earth reveals itself, your true gift of Invisibility will be so welcoming; it is your natural healer.

As a transformational healer, helping to support and encourage others through their own transformation, you will be able to share the importance of not always having to be visible when in service; this is very satisfying. You will see how many will instantly feel uplifted and inspired, and then begin to show more confidence in the way they live their life.

Your own transformation and growth will be mostly invisible for a big part of your journey, but believe me, you will know that your light will be shining, that you are doing enough, as much as the extroverts out there who are being seen. Invisibility really can become your saviour.

Validation is important to all your lessons, especially loving yourself and feeling worthy, knowing you are collectively always making a difference. This is a hugely valuable lesson; sometimes it is the over-looked or forgotten ones who really are and have been an essential part in regards to their Invisibility, helping to clear the way, even set the stage, so to speak, for humanity's ascension. Assisting or transforming the very DNA of humanity to form bridges for other beings, other rays of light, to come forward.

You may feel being invisible is not always going to get you the recognition you deserve. But the reward is the knowledge itself that what you're doing is a special gift. Of course, recognition is great and everyone deserves to receive it during this very emotional journey. The true accolade that you deserve is to really feel worthy, and love yourself unconditionally.

I know for sure I am still being prepared for something amazing in the visible world; it is time to give my Invisible gifts a voice. The world needs more sensitivity, and it is my intention to enjoy going with the flow, allowing all my wonderful opportunities to reveal themselves.

I will truly honour my spiritual sensitivity, to take me to that heavenly place that is inside of me. Knowing I can go inside and be visible there, is beyond my dreams – it is where I do my best work.

Invisibility: this is how I work as a transformational healer; it allows me to use my loving powerful presence to reach out to many, many others, while they embrace their own transformation, revealing their own special gifts.

> *"My work gives me a lightness of spirit, like gently floating on a summer breeze."*
>
> - ANON

Invisibility truly was the catalyst that led me to become a published author, and allowed me to reach out with my powerful messages to inspire and uplift others.

Invisibility helps you to become free, so embrace all opportunities to strengthen your faith, to help other people evolve, bringing hope to humanity.

> *"Flying above on the wings of a dove… feeling peace, feeling free, to Invisibility."*
>
> - DAWN CUMMINS

INVISIBLE

NURTURE

The Power *of* Invisibility

CHAPTER TWO

NURTURE

Nurturing and nourishing yourself, equals loving yourself. Now is the time to truly embrace that nurturing and nourishing, pure unconditional love of self, deep within yourself, expand it into your whole being. Taking good care of yourself plays a huge part in your life purpose. Your life is about now, not tomorrow, it is about being in the moment.

You must take responsibility to nurture yourself; it is paramount for highly sensitive people (or HSPs), Earth Angels, light workers and empaths. Self-care and self-awareness is vital. It plays a huge part in regards to your well-being, and to identifying where your stressors are, then you can take positive action to limit them. You can start by beginning to nourish your inner world: slow down, become more aware and receive your wisdom from within.

Just saying the word 'nurture' can feel challenging for many people. They may feel uncomfortable, not

13

understanding or accepting it to be the most natural gift that is available to us. It is about starting to embrace the love of self, and then receiving it into your heart and accepting that you are worthy of it.

Just like the seeds you plant, they require you to nurture them. Most people find nurturing other things or people much easier than nurturing themselves. This is so typical of carers who are prone to burnout, but usually this is down to not caring for themselves first.

Everyone has the choice to listen to themselves, so begin to start investing in nourishing yourself deeply. Believe too, that the more you take care of your mind, body and spirit, the more you will not only help yourself, but will help others also, to restore and rejuvenate their energy.

The message here is very much in alignment with Invisibility, because divine love is continuously working to keep you nourished, so keep on allowing your heart to open, receive, and be filled with pure love. There is no separation, as divine love is always there for you.

Your spiritual practice, working with energies, nurturing yourself and being in service is a daily routine and a full time commitment. So whether you are an introvert or an extrovert, Invisibility is about feeling nurtured and nourished, which means you need to continue to take care of your energy.

A life review takes courage, looking to see what patterns of behaviour are not serving you. But when you begin to feel, know and see, you don't have to chase after life; you become still, quietening your mind, and you let life come to you.

When you trust and follow your inner guidance, you can help yourself by adjusting your habits to a healthier lifestyle. A healthy lifestyle would involve eating a healthy diet, which then becomes a natural process. Get adequate sleep and exercise, taking care of your body, resting more, having time out, even considering going on a Retreat. Re-energise, re-connect to the deep inside, increasing the level of your well-being to a much more positive outlook, allowing your self-esteem to naturally blossom.

> *"Love joyously, plan thoughtfully*
> *and trust completely."*
> - **ECKHART TOLLE**

Make some lifestyle changes, like time management: start saying "no" to extra responsibilities, worry less, delegate more, enjoy some leisure time. This would be a really good start to introducing a self-care plan, and practising spirituality, giving your mind, body and soul true nourishment – this self-nourishment really can help to shift stuck energy.

This would help bring about a change in your well-being, inviting your body to receive, relax, and release resistance to any energy that actually isn't in harmony with what you want to experience in life.

Your self-care plan would start with honouring yourself and your feelings, respecting and valuing yourself, because you are so deserving. Be gentle and kind to yourself, knowing you are and do enough. Remember to give yourself daily acknowledgement for how hard you work.

Get into practising assertiveness, having those boundaries and never putting yourself last. Boundaries are a form of self-care too, so always focus upon balancing all the giving you do, making sure that you also receive. Allowing yourself to receive is just as important as giving and such a big part of the self-care plan.

Honouring your power, having compassion for yourself, increases self-love. Opening and allowing yourself to connect to the divine love that you already have, it will be the most nourishing thing you will ever do.

"I learned to meet my needs, and not call it selfish."

When I Loved Myself Enough
- ALISON & KIM MCMILLEN

A nurturing plan

This would be about self-care, positive thinking, affirmations, meditation, breathing exercises, grounding your energy, and eating a healthier diet, and would also incorporate what I call my spiritual practice.

A spiritual practice is about self-love, self-care and responsibility for yourself. Nourishing your emotional, mental and spiritual self is always essential to your health and well-being, just as much as nutrition and exercise. It is then about the rituals, and how they will still help in making those changes, giving you huge amounts of support, strength and wisdom, which will lead you to live the life that you deserve.

Positive thinking

You can heal through the power of positivity and love. You can commit to a greater possibility from your life, knowing each time you think a positive thought, you will bring more positive energy to the world. Your positivity really will back up your focus and vision.

> *"Your vision will become clear when you can look into your own heart. Who looks outside, dreams; who looks inside, awakens."*
>
> - **CARL GUSTAV JUNG**

A happy, relaxed, positive person is rewarded as a healthy individual. There is certainly power in positive thinking when you give your full attention to your goals, to promoting the success you are aiming for. Allow the miracles to happen, and the impossible actually does become possible. Change your thoughts, change your world to a new way of living and a new way of thinking.

> *"I am positively focused, always."*

Today can be the start of the rest of your life, because unless you change how you are, you will always get what you have always got. When we focus our intention, not in our heads, but in our hearts, we communicate from the heart level, extending our heart energy with positive emotions of love, compassion and gratitude, then we see those miracles show up in our lives.

Affirmations can be used daily, especially on waking; this is when your sub-conscious door is open.

*"I trust in the magical healing power
of love transforming my life."*

"I feel happy and at peace with myself."

"I am a success in all that I do."

"I live each day with passion and purpose."

*"I choose to use my power, having love and
harmony in all areas of my life."*

"I give myself permission to be powerful."

"I am always connected to source."

*"I have a unique destiny and every day
that path is being revealed to me."*

"With trust, faith and courage I will succeed."

Meditation

Meditation is a process of inward visualisation, ultimately relaxing, and stilling the mind. There is no right or wrong way. Maybe keep it simple to start with, as I feel the reason many people do not meditate is purely because they feel it has to be done in a precise manner, and just the title "meditation" can put them off, maybe because they have read or been told it should be done this way or that way.

Meditation helps make choices for a greater life, so let the universal force align and connect. The key lies in your intention, so to help the process along, it would be great to bring in the positive thoughts like, "I can meditate easily," instead of, "I can't meditate". In so many ways, meditating is a natural part of life, we have just forgotten how. We have learnt to keep filling the gaps, which only adds to stress and anxiety.

Meditation can be something as simple as just going for a walk, either in nature such as the woods or along the beach, or sitting staring at a candle, daydreaming, using your imagination. The results are so beneficial, especially to your overall well-being, and your breathing becomes slower and calmer. It is said that meditation and prayer complement each other, and it is highly recommended to do both often.

A meditation of peace and stillness

Find a comfortable quiet place, ideally sitting with your spine straight, and your feet flat on the ground. Take a few breaths in and out, then return to your normal breathing, starting to feel the tension drain away. Allow the word "peace" to fill your mind.

Now notice your body, how it is feeling; think about your back and begin relaxing your spine; be aware of your breathing, allowing your spine to relax even more.

Thinking about your legs now, see them becoming completely relaxed, then notice your stomach muscles relaxing, and let the tension release from your chest, breathing slowly, easily.

Let this feeling of relaxation spread up into your arms, feel the heaviness reaching to your shoulders. Let them relax, dropping easily, so relaxed.

Feel the peace, the quietness surround you, as the tension melts away from your neck and shoulders, checking that your body is still feeling so relaxed: your feet, legs, spine, stomach, arms, neck and shoulders.

Keep breathing gently and easily, and as you breathe out, relax a little more, no tension, just that complete feeling of quiet and relaxation.

Even your face feels more relaxed as the muscles unwind, letting go of all tensions, as your jaw begins to relax, more and more.

Now feel that all over sensation of really letting go, feeling at peace, the stillness, more restful... just listening to your breath in... and out... as your body becomes heavier, looser and so relaxed.

Enjoy this feeling for a little longer, then slowly start to bring yourself back to where you are sitting. Wriggle your toes, stretch if you need to, even yawn... open your eyes, sit quietly for a minute, then slowly start to move again. Notice that total feeling of peace and relaxation.

This exercise is very beneficial to really experience stillness, peace and tranquillity which will become enhanced as you practise and embrace meditation, and feel how simple it can become.

Prayer

A simple thought, like an affirmation, and the greatest gift you can give. It is very uplifting, giving you that divine connection. Prayer can be a simple thought: a blessing, a good intention coming from your heart, asking that another will be filled with Divine Love. These two prayers below will demonstrate just that, so enjoy.

"ANGEL OF JOY"

"Beloved Angel of Joy, awaken our hearts to the joy of life. Let us love and open ourselves to your presence at all times. Protect the joyful and preserve their innocence. Remind us that our natural state is one of harmony and grace. Help us to re-affirm the pure state of joy in all that we are and all that we do."

"JUST FOR YOU"

"There's no problem too big, and no question too small
Just ask God in faith and he'll answer them all
Not always at once, so be patient and wait
For God never comes too soon or too late
So trust in his wisdom and believe in his word
For no prayer's unanswered and no prayer's unheard."

Breathing Exercises

These help with overcoming fear, anxiety, stress, tension, and also connect you to your feelings. When we are stressed, we tend to unconsciously hold our breath, yet, as you know, breathing is essential to oxygenating your brain, body, mind and spirit, and of course life. Breathe deeply for relaxation and prioritise time for yourself, let it help you engage in something you enjoy, re-charging spiritually, emotionally and physically.

Find a balance in taking in several deep breaths, inhaling positive energy, and then exhaling all negativity. This will awaken your energy, which can also help to release those old thought patterns. So it is important to remember to take some deep breaths throughout your day, as it will help to re-centre you, feeling calmer and more at peace with yourself, leading to having a more loving outlook towards life.

I recommend the 3 Deep Breaths technique; you can do this anywhere and any time. At least once daily would be so beneficial to your health generally, make that commitment to yourself and take those steps, it really is important. The technique is explained below.

So this is what I repeat when I inhale and exhale:

"I breathe in love, light, peace, joy and harmony," and I exhale breathing out: "Love, light, peace, joy and harmony." It feels really good to do and even more relaxing.

Once you become confident in this technique and understand that you inhale positive energy, and then exhale all negativity, you may feel you would like to not only *inhale* the positive energy, but also *exhale* the same positive energy. I wanted to share my own experience with you.

For a long time I have practised inhaling positive and then exhaling negative energy. Perfect for releasing stress or anxiety and becoming calmer and at peace.

But now I find I want to inhale and exhale the same positive energy as mentioned. I have proved to myself that the 3 Deep Breaths technique works, because over time, regular practising of the technique and making it part of your daily ritual gets you to a place where you want to give out the same positive energy – it really does come naturally.

For now I suggest you practise the version of the 3 Deep Breaths technique, you will know if and when you want to add anything different. I still exhale any negative energy that I might be experiencing in some situations, it is still a tool that I can draw on. The importance of breathing correctly and practising it is paramount and will enhance your life.

3 Deep Breaths

Begin by taking your first deep breath in, drawing in the positive energy, and really feeling the love, joy, peace and harmony… then start to let go, exhaling all the negativity. Just let go of any stress, fear, tension and anxiety that you may be feeling, anything that isn't love.

Again, begin to take in the second deep breath, deep into your abdomen, visualise love, light, peace and tranquillity… then exhale, letting go of all the tension in your shoulders, any anxiety, just let it go… let out a big sigh maybe… as you release all the negative energy that has built up, in and around you.

Now for the third deep breath: really feel the positivity, love and light surrounding you, feeling calm… now, as you exhale, let go of everything that does not serve you any more, really let it go.

Notice how much more relaxed and peaceful you're feeling. When you are disciplined and practise your breathing, you really will begin to re-centre yourself and experience the true benefits which are considered to be the most important contribution towards your health and well-being.

"You are never far from the light, it is as close as your breath."

Grounding

Connecting with nature is important to our health and well-being. With such busy lives, we often find less time to spend outside, and even less time for focusing on ourselves. Being able to be outside with nature and connect to the Earth is so grounding; it calms and slows us down, helping us feel less anxious or worried, but gain more clarity in our life as nature really is fuel for the soul.

This short visualisation will help to ground you, but it is also important to do it after you experience any situations where you feel your energy has been drained.

Sit or stand comfortably, ideally with bare feet, making sure both your feet are flat on the ground. Connecting to the Earth outside is best, but indoors is fine too.

You might want to close your eyes as you visualise roots coming out of the soles of your feet, going deep into the earth, just like the roots of a tree... and as they go deeper into the heart centre of Mother Earth, connecting you to your Earth Star. Continue to visualise the energy of pure unconditional love. Now start to bring it back up into your body and into all your energy centres, including your heart, up and out through the top of your head, reaching higher as you connect to your Soul Star: as it is above, so it is below.

Now imagine yourself in a bubble of golden light, feeling safe as you continue with your day.

A healthy diet

This means giving your body nourishing foods and really tuning into your body, knowing what it wants. Get to know what really are the best foods for it, and especially, become aware of foods that are chemical-free. Concentrate on eating food that gives you energy: avoid refined grains, sugars, oils and anything with chemical additions.

Exercise is nourishing too, so taking small steps is always better than taking none at all, but always think towards what suits you personally. Walking, swimming and yoga are more gentle ways to exercise, but are just as nourishing as heavier exercise overall, and help you to stay positive and motivated.

True nourishment is a commitment, but also a choice, and if you really want that vitality back, feeling re-energised and recharged, then it's priceless in the long term.

You can be the expression of radiant health. Your body is the ideal body for you in this lifetime, so start by letting the stream of well-being flow through you now and always, allowing you to experience inner peace and fulfilment.

From a holistic perspective, here are some tips on certain foods which have really helped me on my journey of discovery. Try to integrate them into a new healthy regime.

Foods

Try to replace oils such as corn, vegetable and sunflower with alternatives such as extra virgin olive oil, avocado and coconut.

Carbohydrates such as bread, pasta and pastries are known to adversely affect many, including myself. I have been diagnosed as wheat sensitive, so gluten-free products are recommended. It is advisable to implement such dietary changes as soon as you can, although it can be challenging to start with.

Your sensitivity really does affect other parts of your body, for example, your digestive system and gluten sensitivity being the most common one. The importance of the foods you eat really will play a big part in regards to your whole being.

Of course, it is all part of the healing process that you will endure on your journey, becoming more and more aware of how you can be affected in your everyday life, all due to a combination of dietary and lifestyle habits.

Apparently these are some of the most ageing foods:

Sugar: this is found in so many things that we eat, but the recommendation is to switch to slow-release carbohydrates which we can find in such things as sweet potatoes, beetroot, carrots or almonds.

Salt: for alternative seasonings, switch to herbs, or look for Himalayan or Celtic salt.

Cow's milk: goat's, soya or almond milk are healthier alternatives.

Meat: a better source of protein for our bodies can be found in fish.

Fats and oils: we know saturated fat is no good for us, so switch to soya and eat plenty of raw nuts which contain their own oils.

Other information that may help to assist you in awareness of your body:

Sluggish digestion: beetroot is best for detoxifying inflammation or a teaspoon of turmeric a day, added to your food.

Oxidation, or bringing more oxygen into your body: orange and yellow fruit are good for this.

Hormone imbalance: garlic, pumpkin seeds, and almonds are recommended.

Acid/alkali imbalance: lemon, garden greens such as asparagus, celery, spinach and kale.

All the above suggestions support the nurturing self-care plan. They are all supportive suggestions of love, for those who may need that "shove": Showing How Our Voice Expresses Love.

> *"Ask the angels above to help those who may*
> *need that shove, with a joyful hug from thee.*
> *Nurturing the soul is to become whole, being who*
> *we came here to be, feeling blessed and to inspire*
> *those souls of Divinity."*

NURTURE

VULNERABILITY

The Power *of* Invisibility

VULNERABILITY

*"Vulnerability, why do you follow that
trend, even pretend? When all you have to
do is become its friend."*

**What version of vulnerability do you perceive to be true for
you, positive or negative, or maybe both? It is commonly
known for humans to feel rather exposed, fearful and
uncomfortable around vulnerability, which naturally
affects self-worth, ultimately making you feel more anxious
and stressed. Finding positive coping mechanisms helps to
break down those beliefs into manageable strategies.**

Your vulnerability is shown when you really share from
your soul, allowing those powerful feelings to be known.
The positive effect of this is that you are showing yourself
who you truly are, leading to accepting that vulnerability is
a gift.

So accept that it is ok to be vulnerable; embrace your courage, be your true self, it will be worth it. Take your personal growth beyond your comfort zone, stretch yourself.

It's scary at times, but in a powerful, authentic way. Embrace it and feel it deep in your heart and soul, connecting to a part of yourself that has the courage to feel vulnerable when called for. Vulnerability certainly is a gift, especially in regard to your own journey of self-love and worthiness. It is not only about having compassion for others, but compassion for yourself as well.

True authenticity is about sharing your feelings and experiences, being brave, bold, and really showing your true self, sharing those deep emotions with people who respect you, and who have earned the right to share them, allowing yourself to be transparent and authentic. Honestly, it really does take courage, understanding that your awareness and true authenticity are emerging, noticing as it becomes more apparent to you, and feeling the love for yourself.

In some ways, I feel I have always been authentic and transparent; some might say I have been too open and honest, which I can relate to. But twenty years ago it was a different kind of communication. I was just being me, sharing and learning from experiences. Sometimes you do realise later, that maybe it is best to keep some things close to your heart. But in essence, what I am saying is that it came naturally to me to be vulnerable to a lot of outside influences, which I now know and understand.

I learnt to peel back my layers of insecurity; if I went to events where there were liked-minded people, or situations where I felt I was in a safe environment, then I was usually the one who would find themselves sharing their heart and soul, being vulnerable.

It felt natural to do, and many people considered I was brave, allowing myself to be vulnerable, and would personally come to me and thank me. I always felt I was there for a reason, which seemed to be to show others that it is safe and ok to show their emotions.

I believe I am an Earth Angel doing divine work, and truly knowing what being in service means.

The main exercise and purpose is being able to show emotion, and being that I am a highly sensitive and emotional soul, I cry openly, naturally, authentically, which again is not something everyone else can do in front of others. I really felt I showed others it was actually ok to cry, be vulnerable and not to be embarrassed. I knew that it helped many people and it was my calling, just by some of their comments. It was and still is a time when people are really healing deeply, and needing the support and encouragement to understand being vulnerable is very normal. Huge healings take place when this happens.

As Brené Brown would say, meaningful human experiences are at the core of vulnerability, the heart centre.

I truly understand this and know it to be true, and totally agree from my own experiences. I would hasten to add I am still a work in progress, and still have my challenges regarding being vulnerable but in many totally different circumstances, where I know that I am still being prepared to serve in my own unique way.

My life was always about what I thought others thought of me, or perhaps wanted from me. So I soon learnt and found that vulnerability is definitely the opposite of weakness.

> *"What makes you vulnerable,*
> *makes you beautiful."*
>
> - BRENÉ BROWN

Know that you can show your vulnerability as being a strength, taking only positive outcomes from any situation. That realisation can also help you to embrace another one of your gifts, which is courage; you will feel like you have bucket-loads of it too, so supportive in helping you to trust your intuition when feeling vulnerable.

I am passionate about all the gifts we have, so I have to mention positivity and how it can turn any negative situation when you're feeling vulnerable, into a positive one, which is always so productive, and it really will uplift you.

There can be very low and maybe desperate times, even finding yourself experiencing some physical challenges, or feeling very vulnerable around health issues. I experienced physical vulnerability when I was having a hip joint problem, and found myself expressing this vulnerability by writing this poem:

"I'm having a bit of a blip with my hip.
I am in pain, which is a shame,
but I'm not going to blame the pain, as I know
I have so much to gain.
I am looking in the mirror and feeling rather vain,
seeing only horror from this pain, again and again.
I am now letting go of all the pain that thinks it
can make me lame,
knowing only love can tame this pain.
Hip, hip hooray this is a magical day!!!"

So positive actions, thoughts and feelings can help turn things completely around, giving you the choice to bring joy into any situation.

The negatives of vulnerability can mean many things to some people, such as low self-esteem, being sensitive, shy, introverted, not trusting others. This can make it all very challenging when putting yourself forward, and speaking out could feel excruciating, plus the fear would only add to the intensity of any situation that arose, feeling very uncomfortable and vulnerable. The feeling of vulnerability can lessen when you let go of the fear that controls your actions, and can help you trust more and have faith in all that you do.

Vulnerability really is just another one of those labels that has been created. It is not going to go away, so choose to learn to accommodate your vulnerability by coping and dealing with it differently, starting in a loving way towards yourself. If you choose, you can go from strength to strength, owning it, and be the beautiful soul that you are, while here on Earth.

Vulnerability gives you the ability to truly be vulnerable in amazing authentic ways, sometimes it will be fun… and other times it will make you want to run from all those peering eyes.

Positive and negative experiences will always arise, challenging you too. But you will never be surprised, you will know your strength comes from within, and it truly is no sin.

Simply feel the love in your heart, not in your mind.

"Love is not love, until love's vulnerable."

- THEODORE ROETHKE

VULNERABILITY

INVISIBLE WINGS

INTENTION

The Power *of* Invisibility

INTENTION

Intention is being clear, here on Earth. Focused, and focusing only on what you want, knowing that the real world is within us all, and that you are being the best version of who you can be. We all have choices as to where we place our intention, and those choices are supported by the Universe, as we connect to our soul purpose. You will know when you have found your intention to be true... just by thinking it, and then your focused energy will help you feel uplifted, just how you imagined it to feel and to be. Divine flow is working in your life; recognise the presence of this never-ending flow of divinity working through you, bringing more meaning, purpose and increased faith into every area of your life.

Intention is everything you do, enabling you to be in alignment with your spirit, choosing only pure intentions as you walk your path, recognising that the love force is coming from your heart, knowing you are connected to your soul, doing the work you came here to do at this time on Earth. Intention is living with an open heart, bringing unconditional love to every experience that you may have.

> *"Intention… is the name of the game, no pain…*
> *no gain… just being you."*
>
> - **DAWN CUMMINS**

What is your intention in life? Your intent can help create your future, although your attention is on the present, meaning that your attention must be focused on the actions you take daily, and you then manifest your intentions tomorrow. It is about accepting the present, being in the now, just as it is, and then intending the future as you would truly like it to be. You could even detach yourself from intentions, preventing you from struggling against the present in the pursuit of manifesting your future.

Do you feel clear about what you want, does it feel positive when you think about it? How exciting does it feel, is it giving you hope? Is your true purpose the intention to feel successful in all that you do?

The power of intention and infinity can be everything, belief in your faith and focused intention can help in creating your desired outcomes. You may be willing to change things and create that new life, wanting to have other experiences for the better.

*"What you do every day matters more than what
you do once in a while."*

- GRETCHA RUBIN

So how would it look and feel? Would it be a new home, job
or maybe a relationship? It truly is a process: daring to be free,
believing in yourself, knowing your brilliance, knowing that
you are co-creating your true essence, expressing the divine
love through your unique soul, and lighting up the world
around you, but more importantly, your world within you.

Intention is focusing upon solutions, not problems, and
without a doubt choosing positive thoughts, like freedom and
expansion, instead of negative thoughts of fear and contraction,
and then taking action. You can use harmony as your
intention, asking to be in harmony with your soul's purpose,
and especially in situations for everyone involved, always for
their highest good.

There is power in visualising your desired life! It is
important to regularly visualise the outcomes you want. To
supercharge your intentions, add the feeling of love into those
visualisations. Anything done with love has so much more
power.

"Today, focus upon balancing all that you do to make sure
that you also receive and take care of yourself."

Your vision will start to become clearer only when you can
look into your own heart.

Meditate, identify with the infinite spirit within. Visualise, celebrate the manifestations of your intentions, surrender and trust, let go of any outcome, let go and let God.

> *"Imagination… is the preview*
> *of life's coming attractions."*
> **- ALBERT EINSTEIN**

A good way to keep your intention the centre of your life is to pick a physical symbol, so it reminds you daily. Remember, once you set your intentions, practice becomes second nature, just by doing a little every day.

The decisions you make and each action that is taken are aiming for that purpose or goal, knowing that your intention creates reality. With pure intent and desire, you then create a firm resolve, which guides your planned actions. Trust that the Universe will take care of the results, while your intention continues to help in creating the miracles that are the natural order of the Universe.

An intention affirmation, before sleep:

> *"I now return to the expanded nature*
> *of love that I am."*

When you wake up first thing in the morning is the best time for your positive intentions, then they will set you up for the day. Your intent, your plan or your purpose is your state of mind and your determination.

"Pray about your intentions asking them to manifest in your life, banish doubt and trust your intuitive feelings, allowing you to clear a space for the power of intention to flow through, lovingly and firmly transforming your intentions."

- DR WAYNE DYER

Have the intention of not worrying and being concerned, not always listening to other people's stories, but begin to start living your own. Strengthen the power of your intentions, always add the feeling of love and inspiration into your visualisation, which of course is important. See yourself doing well, using positive visualisations, and you will do well; imagine that you already have your true desires when you go within.

"We have intention and purpose within us."

- OPRAH WINFREY

"God, as I use the word, is another name for what is. I always know God's intention. It is exactly what is in every moment."

- BYRON KATIE

My personal intention for you is to live a life of joy. Let your words be with attention, intent, feeling and visionary.

For many years now I have owned a very special book, called *Praying with Power* by José Luis Stevens. In many ways, it's like a bible may be to others. I am going to share this prayer:

PRAYER FOR INTENT

Spirit, you intended for me to be here,
and so I am here.
Spirit, you intended for me to wake up,
so I am waking up.
Spirit, you intended for me to become a co-creator,
so here I am.
Now I am intending to intend what you intend.
I am intending to know you better.
I am intending to be here fully present.
I am intending to awaken.
I am intending to experience you every single moment.
I am intending to be powerfully conscious.
I am intending to be blessed. I am intending to be a
singer and a dancer.
I am intending to be free at last.
I am intending to be joyful.
I am intending to be loving and to be loved.
I am intending to make a difference.
I am intending to be a participant.
I am intending to complete my contribution.
I am intending to serve with gladness.
I am intending to be rich with resources.
I am intending to be wise.
I am intending to be perfectly healthy.
I am intending to be fully charged with essence.
I am intending to spread peace and light.
I am intending to die with a big grin on my face,
because I lived my life with complete abandon.

And I lived with my heart full and spilling over.
Spirit, my intent is your intent.
And whatever I see in my life is what we intend
together from now on.

I really hope you enjoyed this beautiful prayer, as it is my true intention for you to embrace it into your heart.

INTENTION

SENSITIVITY

The Power *of* Invisibility

SENSITIVITY

Sensitivity, where do I begin? I will start with one of my poems:

"It is part of the frame… from where I came…
you know, from that plain, the same…
as where you came from, too.
So here I go with a line or two, to explain that it
doesn't have to be a strain.
Sensitive… is really ok, so just… be okay.
Sensitive… always doing your best…
And yes, it could be a test, of your integrity.
So join the rest, but let them see
how sensitivity is a wonderful gift,
that supports you in the best possible way.
Sensitive… this may be true,
but it could be you, so just wait and see.
It will help you to grow and show you how
positivity can help you to go with the flow.
Only you know your deep inner strength,
how it can take you to incredible lengths of strength,
as you continue to embrace your true integrity."

"Are You a Sensitive Soul, focusing on your goal, pursuing the truth from within?"

Sense…it…I've spells exactly that: you sense it. When you have a highly sensitive nature, sensing and feeling energy is more apparent to you. Sensitivity is a beautiful and powerful spiritual gift that helps you discern your inner truth. So, as you allow yourself to distinguish from a degree of sovereignty, you then start to liberate your psychic senses, which is your intended purpose for your sensitive gifts. Many highly sensitive souls are aware that they may seem different, so allow yourself to re-think and embrace your sensitivity. Honour it, always see it as a strength, feel empowered, see it as a perceptive ability. Intending to focus on becoming more sovereign and identifying yourself as you develop your awesome gifts of perceptual openness.

What are Empaths or HSPs? HSP stands for highly sensitive people. Empaths have the same qualities: they can feel emotions, both positive and negative, and sense others' feelings, but without absorbing those feelings into their own minds and hearts, as they would both suffer from over-stimulation. So very often they tend to avoid social contact because of the possibility of overwhelm. Silence and stillness are both paramount for them, re-charging their energy, and retreating often is essential.

Maybe you are a Highly Sensitive Person, and an ultra-sensitive Empath to the energies and emotions right now, so honour yourself and your feelings on your unique path. Your presence of being is a gift of amazing frequency to the Earth and humanity, helping to re-establish the empathic resonance to earth, nature and the Universe.

HSPs may be seen as weak, but their strength is different, it can be very powerful. Sensitive emotions can, through creative expression, help others who have similar feelings. Adults and children especially need support with their sensitive emotions. HSPs make ideal counsellors and healers; their presence can change the energy in a room, an event or a situation to a place of peace and calmness.

Acceptance is huge, and it is very much a lesson for you to accept that you are different, but in a loving caring way. Sensitivity can cause pain at times, mentally, emotionally and physically, but it is important to understand that there is no such thing as being too sensitive. Sensitivity is a beautiful, priceless gift. The positives of being a sensitive or an empath is for you to know and believe that you contribute to making the world a better place; you uplift others' spirits by saying the exact words, cheering them up.

To deal with your sensitivity regarding the opinions of others, just accept how you feel, because the more you resist your feelings, the more negative you will become. Consciously make a choice not to hold onto that negativity. If and when possible, remove yourself physically from all negative environments, only interact with positive likeminded, spiritual people. Every empath is an HSP, but not every HSP is an empath. Empaths are known to have more challenges, plus you either are or you are not an empath, it is certainly not a trait that you learn, I feel you are born with the gift. The main goal of an empath is to become comfortable living this way.

The word "empathy" was my first experience of having some understanding, and was introduced to me when I studied and qualified as a counsellor. The explanation was "expressing how you would put yourself in someone else's shoes, really knowing and feeling their emotions with true compassion". Counsellors, healers and carers are natural Earth Angels, showing their kindness and thoughtfulness in caring, empathic ways.

For an empath, it is vitally important to start living with recognition of which energy is their own and which energies have come from other people, which they have absorbed, affecting them, making them feel unwell, very drained, and often not understanding why. Continually ask yourself, "Does this emotion belong to me?" and when you find yourself absorbing another person's negative emotion, take a deep breath in, see or visualise pure white light, then release those emotions as you exhale, allow your angels in and ask that they transmute those unwanted energies into the light, and really feel the love and peace that comes.

My experience of my own transformational healing journey of self-exploration and personal development was definitely choosing to peel back my vulnerable layers of insecurity. I soon found I became much more sensitive around energies in general, and felt this was showing and guiding me to become more disciplined around my self-care, knowing I still needed to learn how to take care of myself in a different way.

My sensitivity is supported by Invisibility, it helps me to live my purpose. I have written about this in the beginning of the book, stating how it is actually crucial to your well-being, and honouring Invisibility. The realisation that I was an empath, who was also a highly sensitive person was in some ways comforting, it explained a lot of un-answered questions that I had.

Most empaths are introverts, private people who choose to help themselves by taking responsibility for their own actions. Empaths have huge hearts and highly tuned senses, so nerves can get very frayed by noise, affecting the nervous system which becomes exhausted. They most certainly have special needs; honouring those needs, and communicating their needs to their loved ones is a priority.

Many introverts are highly intuitive, and need time alone to recharge, retreat. This actually becomes part of your daily routine or rituals as we all now seem to understand. A huge lesson for myself, which I am still embracing and learning, is coming to terms with the way my life has become, actually living my true purpose, owning who I truly am with the passion of that pure love inside of me, unconditional love.

A strong time-management plan is paramount, where meditation and nature can help to replenish you. Set limits and boundaries with people that drain you.

Very often, empaths are quiet achievers, allowing Invisibility to be the key in helping them achieve it. This is an example of understanding the true essence of the power of Invisibility.

Everything around us is energy, so when you come into contact with humans, you will always most certainly be open to picking up on their energy, including issues that might be going on for them, positive or negative. Their energy can have a profound impact on you, you will feel their pain and sadness as your empathic nature will allow your innate ability to intuitively feel and perceive others' emotions. Unconsciously, your life is influenced by others' desires and wishes, so even more reason to implement a strong self-care regime, to have in place always. The importance of creating a totally new lifestyle will ultimately be supporting and accommodating you to maintain yourself, taking care of your well-being first and foremost.

Understanding how Invisibility plays an important role is crucial to how you manage your own energy, because empaths can perceive physical sensitivities, as well as just knowing the intentions and motivations of other people. Your body is a trustworthy instrument of measurement, indicating your tolerance levels, steering you clear of that which your body signals you to avoid.

You need to acknowledge your heightened sensitivity to energies and emotions, realising the truth of your being, as you learn how to thrive in a world that may overwhelm you. You might be known as anti-social, weird, weak and fragile, all negative comments we know, and yes, I believed them to be true on my own journey of discovery, until becoming who I truly am.

Comments of such low energy are so limiting, and will obviously affect people's confidence generally, but for HSPs, empaths, whether introvert or extrovert, you will be challenged to delve deeper to resolve those confidence issues. The focus is all about your alignment to becoming whole. Being clear, believing you are far greater than you perceive, always considering how you really feel.

Embrace and honour your feeling of sensitivity, seeing it as a strength and trusting it, knowing what a wonderful gift it is, helping you make a difference in the world, letting sensitivity be your barometer, indicating that you will know when some situations are not right. You have many amazing gifts. Sensitivity really has to be one truly treasured gift, especially regarding your life lessons and helping others, serving you well.

Learn to accept that you can shine from that quiet place within, without having to be an extrovert to do that. Be encouraged to live your life with true self-confidence and self-appreciation. Being human is meant to be a dream: it's what you wanted, choosing to be here, it's your free will, thriving to be the best you can be, as there is no one like you.

Due to sensitivity, being an introvert and having that empathic nature, the key here is to always balance your needs. It takes courage to be yourself, to be transparent, using self-expression through your amazing presence, sharing your unique gifts, genuinely living fully as the Divine Light that you are.

You will discover immense capacity opening up for you, leading life on the edge at times, in alignment with much vaster fields, stepping forth to express the gift of your sensitive nature, paving the way for others to do the same. Life on the edge needs those that have highly sensitive perceptions to really step forward and express themselves fully. You are on your path of ascension which will call for heightened awareness, and with this awareness comes new levels of sensitivity. Keep on shedding your limiting ideas of who you are and what you can do, to commit to the freedom, furthering your development in this life.

Your incredible differences are your gifts to the world, so your way to freedom is by total acceptance of them. It is letting yourself experience these frequencies, gently and without resistance, anchoring these energies in your body, becoming your reality, knowing all is well. As you accept all of yourself, you will grow and love all other parts of yourself, leading you to that wholeness of expansion, receiving more of all that you require to live in the world, really feeling total joy and love within yourself.

*"May your sensitivity be a blessing to
yourself and others."*

SENSITIVITY

INTUITION

The Power *of* Invisibility

INTUITION

"The intuitive mind is a sacred gift, and the rational mind, its faithful servant. We have created a society that worships the servant, and dismisses the gift."

- ALBERT EINSTEIN

This is so true when coming to trusting our own inner guidance, tending to get stressed over so much more information that is available, instead of using the natural gift that is within us all, which is also available to us all the time. Our heads get overloaded, just like when we refer to our computers being overloaded; it's no different, and, yes they will crash eventually too, if we keep pushing ourselves. It is knowing when we are done, becoming aware of the signs. We need to actually stop, breathe deeply and most importantly, listen, and draw on that inner strength. It is so easy to dismiss our intuition, that great gift that only needs to be listened to – not sometimes, but always.

*"Trust your inner feelings to tell you the truth,
even if it's difficult to hear the honest answer."*

- ANON

Understand the nature of your intuition, which enables you to make decisions in the immediate moment, from the emotional, psychological and spiritual components of any given situation, which are the here-and-now ingredients of life. We underestimate our inner knowing, our intuition. It has been undervalued, but it is our natural coping gift. It is our inner tutor!

Our thoughts and experiences also help us to interpret inspiration, the spiritual wisdom available to us from within. This wisdom is often like a small voice calling way out in the wilderness, drowned by our critical and judgmental thoughts.

As a culture we have learned to believe that rationality is what prevails when making decisions. It bridges the gap between the conscious and the non-conscious parts of our mind, and also between instinct and release. In essence, we need both to make the best possible decisions for ourselves. Our natural ability or power, intuitively or instinctively, makes it possible to know something without proof.

Intuition is a process that gives us the ability to know something directly without any analytical reasoning. Instinct is an inclination, or gut feeling, a sensation that appears quickly. Sadly, many have been led to ignore them, even dismiss what they can't prove; this is a shame because it is not trusting the guidance from their inner wisdom. Intuition is inner wisdom, knowing and trusting it will guide your choices; it's directly connected to your heart, not your head or intellect. It really is that hidden ingredient that will transform a challenge or situation into a positive advantage, so attune your wise centre, balancing it with your silent knowing.

*"I open myself to the wisdom within,
knowing that there is only one intelligence
in this Universe."*

The question we all want answered is, how do we know if that voice is coming from our inner wisdom, or maybe from emotions of fear? From personal experience as I have already mentioned earlier, when you know, you just know.

Spiritually, this is known as clairsentience, (a clear feeling), and claircognizance, (a clear knowing); both are inner knowing, just knowing something without logic. Both help your ability to receive intuitive messages. You are and have the capacity to be a conduit for information and wisdom; pray to receive clarity and know it to be true.

Signs that can also clarify that your knowledge comes from your inner wisdom, could certainly be just feeling calm, peaceful and positive. If you have reactive responses which feel negative due to old patterns which were guided by emotions of fear, or even anger, then possibly they are not going to be productive in the long run.

The message would be "trust your vibes"; you know they are coming from your heart, so when you do pick up on those vibes, then really trust them. Let them direct and guide you in ways that only serve your highest good, always. Allow your heart to expand by trusting your vibes, and see your stress dissolve all around you, as your heart expresses even more love.

> *"Hold in your heart... the true place of understanding... a stillness which is alive ... like the heart of a rose."*

Truly embrace the vibrancy of trusting, and then feel the joy and enthusiasm from within. With practice, your inner guidance does get stronger; it opens up your heart, aligning you with more love, not fear. Let the pure, unconditional love in, touching your intuition as you live by it, and your inner wisdom, love and light will lead you to true freedom. Keep inviting intuition into your heart and really falling in love with life.

> *"I trust and listen to my intuition, it will lead me to love."*

Live authentically, as life is meant to be an authentic experience. Spend time in nature as you follow your intuition, it helps in opening up to an even more natural and authentic human being, that strength and power that resides within each of us, re-connecting with nature and your natural self. Honour your true feelings, stand up for what you know to be true, deep in your heart, and always listen to the voice of your highest and most authentic self, living a heartfelt life, full of purpose. It is your heart that wants to take risks maybe, so be bolder than what your rational mind might actually allow, as the path you seek is right before your eyes.

Allow yourself to be completely transparent, accepting who you really are, finding the courage to share all the parts of you that make you unique, and do it your way. Without any outside influence, but only trusting your true inner self to be the best you can be, there really is no one else like you. You become your true essence, shining that diamond from within.

Trust yourself, be in the flow. It is about finding that inner stillness just for a few minutes, and really listening for a message, waiting in silence, holding the attitude of growth and steady development, which can then transform your own understanding. Unleash your natural powers, you have an important life purpose, it is time to own it, and time to assume your leadership power, lovingly guiding others.

Create a deeper connection, and pay attention, tap into your internal spiritual guidance that is being offered to you from the Universe; it will raise your vibration, expanding your perspective on life. Intuition is always there, available to us all the time. Some might say you have stopped looking for it, not paying attention to it. Trusting and knowing what you know to be true is simple, because when you know, you know.

"The only obstacles standing in your way are the fears in your mind. Release your fears and you release the obstacles."

Your inner voice knows the truth, the feelings and having the sense of knowing. Another expression is known as your sixth sense, which links you to your inner world from the inside out, not always logical or even making sense, you just know. It can show up in dreams, positive or negative vibes, and there will be coincidences, gut feelings too. Pay attention to your gut feelings, they are signals of your truth. You will get physical responses to your knowing, goose bumps could be an example. Spontaneity is also about intuition, because when it feels right, be guided to do just that. The more you act on your inner guidance or intuition, the more power and clarity you will receive, as you truly are a resource for the Universe or your source energy.

My experience of working with my intuition, is the very important key of positivity, letting it guide me, feeling confident in knowing I am doing the right thing in any given situation.

"Trust your feelings and inner knowing
to tell you the truth."

Then harmony starts to develop as you continue to follow your trustworthy guidance. Synchronicities start to occur, allowing the magic to happen, all due to you taking action on that intuitive strength from your inner guidance, where the connections really happen.

Intuitive people are more often introverts, as they like to take time for solitude and silence anyway. They enjoy plenty of down time, practising mindfulness, and with practise connect more naturally to their intuition.

> *"Intuition… expresses the magic of fruition,*
> *it blows you away. It is intense, so don't stay*
> *sitting on the fence… because, remember the other*
> *day, that replay… that intuitive hunch, you know*
> *the one just before lunch."*

Mindfulness is important too, letting go of negative emotions, quieting the mind, creating, observing and connecting more deeply to that abundant divine flow. All the meditating and breathing exercises mentioned in Chapter Two, Nurture, will help to achieve this. Anything that you feel will help you, allowing your mind to relax, re-connecting with yourself.

We all receive our own personal guidance, it may be telling you to be more at peace within your heart, your life, your home. At times if you feel you have lost that connection, take time to be still, silent and just "be" for a while, until your mind settles. Take that lovely walk you keep promising yourself, connect with nature, or gaze at the clouds in the sky, even listen to some soothing music, whatever feels good for you. Your intention is key, as there is no right or wrong way, only your way.

INTUITION

INVISIBLE WINGS

BELIEVE

The Power *of* Invisibility

BELIEVE

I believe we all have our place on this planet, choosing to learn our life lessons.

Although Dr Wayne Dyer's quote expresses perfectly how we may hinder those lessons:

"There is one grand lie: that we are limited. The only limits we have are the limits we believe."

Don't you just know and believe that to be true? We beat ourselves up, and yes, limit our true potential. Limiting thoughts like, believing others do so much more than we do, are better than us, because they seem to be out there and visible.

I chose that to be true too, because I believed I had to be visible to be worthy of my gifts. So believe in your thoughts, knowing them to be true. My realisation was that my ascension path was to heal on a much deeper level, my identity of self-love and worthiness.

Here is a powerful affirmation for you to repeat, when you feel lesser than:

"I am now choosing to rise above all limitations."

Dissolving our limiting beliefs will shift any perception, opening you up to greater love. Sometimes, once you realise, accept or let go of a limiting belief that isn't true, you feel happier, feeling the love, freedom and expansion in your heart.

There is always value in your experiences when you believe that everything is possible, believing the more you receive, the more you can help others, to then taking that action, releasing the need to believe as others do. You can be the one who remembers, believing the power of who you truly are, and your ability to reach your goal, believing your action is divinely guided always.

Trust in your strength, your faith and believe in yourself, willing to commit to listening and discovering your soul voice. Have a clear vision, harness your suppressed spirituality; hearing those secrets of your voice with true dedication from within takes courage.

When you believe with your whole heart, you can accomplish any task. It is your most powerful motivator, it will help you overcome any doubt or fear, strengthening your faith, uplifting and empowering you as you become more at peace with yourself, to enjoying a much more joyful outlook. Feel the passion, feel more enthusiastic, inspired and truly believing you are making a difference in the world.

Do you have dreams, do you believe in miracles? If not why not? They can and do come true when you believe.

I believe in the healing power of sound vibration. We are sound vibration. Do you believe that, do you know if it's true? The choice is that we don't have to believe everything we read anyway. So if you are inspired by music or sound, I would love to share with you singer-songwriter Emeli Sandé's album, *Long live the Angels*. I love all the tracks but I am inspired by the second one, *Breathing Underwater.* It is very powerful, and starts with the words, "I believe in miracles".

Believing is in tune with your intuition and knowing, you can feel that strength in your heart and soul. Remove all self-doubt, never stop believing, dreaming, learning or trying and never give up, but know and believe you can achieve the impossible.

Believe in the power from within, stay positive, call upon the angels, keep the faith, allowing yourself to receive these contributions to living your life purpose. Believe in holding your faith, believe the trust, have full confidence, to believe and express your understanding of truth.

Definitions of belief vary; it could simply be, do you believe in God, angels or ghosts, or do you believe in daily exercise? It could be that water is good for you because our bodies are made up of 80% water, or it could be I don't believe everything I read, they didn't believe me. Or it could be about believing that you will have much more time later.

"Belief" is such a complex word. Would you say believing is true and honest? I like to believe so, as I feel this chapter on Believe is positive.

Sometimes negativity can come from believing, if we give credit to the testimony or authority of another, somehow finding ourselves being persuaded of their truth – which is their belief only – as believing in another seems easier to put confidence in them, more than we actually would for ourselves. Never let anyone make you believe that you have to be anything less than the best version of who you really are.

This verse below is worth pondering over, and with belief, take these words into your heart.

BEYOND BELIEF

Whether or not you believe in God, is for you alone to know.
But be assured that if you do, God's love for you will show.
For where before you may have lived your life in
a selfish way,
The change that God will bring about,
will enrich your everyday.
Your past so filled with darkness and depression of the mind,
Will be replaced by God's true light, a blessing you will find.
And as you put your trust in God, and see what he can do,
You'll know such love and joy and peace to fill your life anew.
God's love for you and me today is a free gift of God's grace,
That reaches beyond barriers of things like time and place.
If you would just believe in Him, then God will do the rest,
For he will guide and strengthen you
… and your life will be blessed.

The Journey of Life
- JOHN B. KNIGHT

BELIEVE

INVISIBLE WINGS

LOVE

The Power *of* Invisibility

LOVE

As soon as I started to think about writing this next chapter, I started humming these lyrics from the Beatles:

"Love, love, love… There's nothing you can do that can't be done, it's easy.

All you need is love, love, love … love is all you need!"

I am feeling so grateful for these words, because I know my purpose is love, my message is love, I am a messenger of love. God is love, I am love, expanding that love out and reaching many others. Divine love flows to and through us, and when we focus only on love, we are then strengthened by love. We are the ambassadors of love releasing that most precious gift we have been given, that gift of love that is connected to our soul.

Every day we are working towards fulfilling our life's purpose, and our promise to the divine love, which really does have lots of time for us all. It shows us that we are attracting more and more love into our life, wanting to live a life pursuing happiness, a fearless love and not settling for anything less. The resilience of that inner love of self was certainly my own experience. Understanding our heart is the portal of love when working on unfolding those layers, opening us up and letting it be our intention and focus for our purpose. Love really does matter and it is the essence of all things, it is the answer.

> *"Wake at dawn with a winged heart, and give thanks for another day of loving."*

Is loving yourself your life's work? Are you worthy of love? Love is doing what makes you happy... there isn't anything in the Universe that isn't love. Love isn't just how we feel for others, it is who we are, that ocean of love flowing within for us to enjoy. It is a love filled with joy that we give and see in each other and the world. It is the source of all that is... love, love, love, it's easy, love is all you need. I can't get the song out of my mind! I feel you already know the best direction to take, so it is important to give yourself permission to follow that path.

Today, tell yourself: "I love you, and I promise to take good care of you."

It most certainly is an inside job, and always starts with ourselves as we evolve. We help others evolve too, as we are all part of the whole, as one, humanity, the collective consciousness. Evolving ourselves in this unique way is really about getting on with it, as we go through life's challenges. Let love bring you back to your true self, as you are naturally infinite.

Choose love over fear always, it creates confidence and purpose; really honour the true love from within, your god-self, as you enter into your mission towards freedom, where you will no longer need to look outside of yourself to find unconditional love. We all seem to lose touch with the unconditional love that is so naturally ours for the taking.

> *"Find the love you seek by first finding the love within yourself, learn to rest in that place within you that is your true home."*
>
> **- SRI SRI RAVI SHANKAR**

Another inspiring quote; you really can go to that deep, inner powerful world, where you have everything you need.

We know sound is a vibration, equally love is also a vibration that makes you magnetic to all that is good and true. So focus on ideas you love, dreams that you love, all things you love and what will inspire you. Practise positivity and being grateful, for example, I am grateful for the beautiful sunshine. Be positive around love too. I love my family, I love my body, I love walking, I love my garden, I love my life!

Love is this strong inner connection, a stillness that you nurture. You will know it by recognising you are more aware to listening in a more profound way. It is empowered love, and things will go on around you as the flow of life continues. Your inner love can and will begin to affect the world directly, as part of the invisible connection starts to begin unleashing your love. You begin to shape your inner world even more, so connect, feel and listen from your powerful inner world.

> *"Love the world as your own self, then you can*
> *truly care for all things."*
>
> **- TAO TE CHING**

The normal approach to love has been, and can be seen as quite self-centred, as we tend to give love in order to receive love, that is, putting conditions on love. But when you can say "no" to someone or a situation, knowing you may be seen as selfish, unkind or awkward, but if it comes from your heart always, that is truly loving yourself.

Loving unconditionally means to let go of past grievances, not giving fear any power, always replacing it with love, and being in the present, not the past.

> *"We are not held back by the love we didn't*
> *receive in the past, but by the love we're not*
> *extending in the present."*
>
> **- MARIANNE WILLIAMSON**

So true, don't you think? It is about bringing love alive; breathe it, think it, feel it and sing it; give love a voice. This opens your heart, letting love into every cell of your body, it is time to open the heart to ourselves. I have noticed there are so many verses and quotes that I have shared, telling me how global the message of love has been and is now radiating out into infinity.

Here is part of a description of one woman's healing journey:

> *"Beneath the tears, she discovered love, tenderness,*
> *and a fullness of being, feelings of her inner*
> *defences against early unsustainable suffering,*
> *that had never been fully permitted. For many on*
> *their journey, this is the inner work of all healing,*
> *to uncover the heart, layer by painful layer."*
>
> **- MARC IAN BARASH**

Unconditional love is the core of all life, the sun shines equally on us all, whoever we are. When we can experience the unconditional nature of love, we then open up to unlimited healing power.

Sometimes love is simply a need for affection based on conditions, which I am sure many can relate to.

If you give to me, I will love you.

If you do as I say, I will love you.

If you are nice to me, I will love you.

Eventually after some challenging lessons and experiences, we do learn to love unconditionally. The opposite challenge is to learn to love yourself unconditionally, possibly harder because you have to get past all self-loathing, low self-esteem, and lack of forgiveness for not being perfect.

An important aspect of loving yourself is the experience of knowing you are loved, and allowing that love to emerge from the inside out. I feel for sure there is always that question in our hearts and minds: what comes first, learning to love yourself or learning to love others? Letting love in or loving yourself? The only way to truly love is to be loved first, this is how we learn about love.

People, even animals who have not been shown love, are often mean, unkind, angry and even unresponsive. But the positive is that maybe even if you have not been shown love from a young age, it is definitely possible to become a loving person, because all love begins with yourself.

> *"Whatever you are doing, love yourself*
> *for doing it. Whatever you are feeling,*
> *love yourself for feeling it."*
> **- THADDEUS GOLAS**

To help this to happen, it is necessary to recognise at the deeper levels, that love is the substance of creation, in every particle of the Universe. Some might say: if this is true, how can so many feel unloved? I feel through my own experiences, it really is that old adage: like the nose on your face, it's right in front of us, but we are too busy looking past it and can't find it.

It is through our ignorance or just believing the illusion that love is something external, we look and think we will find happiness from those outside influences.

Don't get me wrong, of course seeing a beautiful sunset or yes, even smelling the roses, (start now, as love sits in the centre of the rose), will make you feel happy. But when you truly start to heal from within, feeling that love – for me it is a divine spiritual love, yes a sacred love – then you begin to understand, or feel true happiness. Then that sunset or rose will have a much more profound meaning to life.

Love is found at the very core of awareness, discovering it is to learn to look within. I know it is such a cliché, but so true to you becoming you. It is not something we are taught to do. My understanding is our life lessons are for that very reason: we came here to learn them and in doing so, achieve that wonderful gift of love of self.

"Love is the answer, you are the source. When I feel connected, I know love is all around, but when I felt separate, I couldn't find love. Then I realised: to experience love is to know it is deep inside of me.

*"I am floating on a bed of love.
I am loving, I am loved."*

- JOSÉ LUIS STEVENS

The definition of love in its purest form of spiritual expression, and particularly unconditional love, is believed to have six aspects, and the highest love is known as:

AGAPE. This means spiritual love, the way God loves you. God is your strength, the love of God is inside of you, you are God. When you understand this love, you give yourself permission to be authentic, transparent, letting life support you, feeling that glow of the powerful sun energy, that warmth inside. It will rejuvenate you, you will float on a bed of pure love, feeling connected and accepting yourself as this being of love and light, feeling safe, joyful, becoming the beautiful soul that you are.

PHILIA is sometimes referred to as a brotherly love, found in friendships.

CHARIS is a love defined by grace, kindness and nurturing from the heart.

EUNOIA is love in action, in service, community, charitable work, deep compassion and commitment.

STORGE is love with tenderness, caring and empathy.

EROS represents romantic physical love, in which souls come together in the union of their bodies.

Maybe knowing these ancient words might change your own definition of what love is.

> *"There is a life-force within your soul, seek that life.*
> *There is a gem in the mountain of your body,*
> *seek that mine.*
> *O, traveller, if you are in search of truth,*
> *don't look outside, look inside yourself, and seek that."*
>
> **- MEWLANA JALALUDDIN RUMI**

LOVE

EMPOWERMENT

The Power *of* Invisibility

EMPOWERMENT

Our inner teacher is what understanding self-empowerment is all about, and a helpful reminder that life is a huge school, as we learn from experiences given to us in every moment. It is the result of our personal and spiritual development, which certainly does define self-mastery, and of course becoming the master of our own destiny. Continue to find that passion for living in the moment, from those choices that will be made from your inner awareness.

I love helping others find their inner potential; I am also passionate about encouraging them to be the best they can be, I help them create their own sense of empowerment because I feel, as a spiritual teacher, you personally become empowered through your own healing journey.

"When I listen to my inner self, I find the answers I need."

Questions that are empowering are positive, but negative questions are so dis-empowering, they are unworthy, keeping you in victim mode and only giving you negative answers, and of course, will get in the way of any positive solutions. Practise thinking only worthy questions, or if a negative one does pop into your mind, immediately replace it with an empowering one; say to yourself, "What can I get from this?"

These are powerful times, so do not judge your challenges as something you have done wrong, or even something you have not yet overcome. It is still about experiencing them, allowing any emotional reaction. But continue moving through them, as you will be fully equipped. Yes, you will see humanity experiencing challenges; just observe, and of course, observe yourself also. Value your connections between humanity and nature and find that neutral part of yourself. Go within to your empowered compassion, it has that powerful effect, even though it can very often be Invisible. When you hold the focus of your empowerment, you are then more conscious of working with the Invisible.

Your consciousness is being in a state of awareness of one's existence, thoughts and sensations, anything that we are aware of at any given moment, which forms part of our consciousness. So personal empowerment is about looking at who you are and becoming more aware of yourself as a unique individual. Set realistic goals, honour your skills and values, fulfil your potential, and know everyone has strengths and weaknesses.

So often, many people under value or even remain unaware of their true abilities.

We talk about being and feeling empowered, not giving our power away. This is a process of becoming stronger and developing more confidence. I totally agree with this as regards embracing our well-being, our spiritual well-being, as I believe we are all spiritual beings, having a human experience, not a human having a spiritual experience. Feel empowered, be the spiritual being that you already are.

Spirituality is not about religion, but it is about being in touch with your divine inner self, your true self on all levels. Our greatest source of empowerment is knowing who we are, so reach out, empower your soul, let it guide you to your goal, fulfil your worth bringing peace on earth, nurturing your soul within.

To be spiritually empowered is about living fully in the moment, learning to love yourself without judgment. Surrender your thoughts over to the divine spirit or God, re-unite with that true love, your love essence that is always within. Think less, feel more, as your body will always know the truth, through intuition, nourishment, meditation, all commitment to your awareness. As you serve and share the love, the Universe will reward you in magical ways, through true empowerment and personal responsibility.

The word spiritual can alarm or make people feel uncomfortable, as it can conjure up many concerns around religious ceremonies or practices. However spirituality has nothing to do with any of that. It's about awakening the consciousness that we humans have all been gifted with. The consciousness is to recognise the truth "about self", about relationships of self, with people and nature. This consciousness helps us to understand and become aware of ourselves and all things that have an impact on our well-being, our inner peace and happiness.

This awareness is empowering because it is the beginning of taking care of our own self, as well as understanding others in a better way. Only when you know who you really are, and what you really want for your ultimate happiness, can you begin to make choices consciously to create realities that would then result in your true happy self. It's only then that you begin to appreciate the need of others to be happy too.

This consciousness of the need to be awakened applies to most of the systems of society, whether education, or any other society or culture; they have all been created without giving regard to this valuable aspect of spirituality, or the needs of the soul. This is resulting in our minds being conditioned, by current educational systems, traditional parenting, or religious preaching. Instead of thinking of a way to help us to get in touch with our "self", it does a good job of taking us further away from ourself. The further away you are from your "inner truth" or your "true self", the more powerless you become, and therefore more vulnerable to exploitation and all things that are capable of eroding your self-confidence and self-esteem.

When we try to control life, we are removed from presence, and act in ways that separate us from others, and solidify the experiences of being an insecure-self. Get comfortable with receiving life, connecting with life, even when someone doesn't feel connected to you, remember it's not personal... keep on connecting.

> *"Spiritual empowerment... is a heart that is ready for anything."*
>
> **- TARA BRACH**

Many of us are on this path of ascension, and are being called or nudged big time towards this new internal empowerment. It is about remembering all you have learned, and integrating it within your being, using your lessons to empower your life now, as they have brought you to where you are today: embrace the gratitude.

> *"I am receiving inner guidance"*
>
> *"I am receiving more love"*
>
> *"I am receiving all the support that is available to me in all areas of my life"*
>
> *"I am grateful for all that I receive"*

Be spiritually empowered by starting where you are, think less, feel more, be committed to live with awareness, be bold, take risks, create community.

Integrating Invisibility, nurturing your soul, feeling vulnerable, with focus and intention, embracing your sensitivity, trusting your intuition, believing in yourself, loving yourself and feeling worthy, can guide you on your ascension journey, continuing to show you the level of internal empowerment and the importance of our own empowered sovereignty, all lessons in empowering your life and trusting the Divine Plan.

Empowerment is about your identity, vision, inner guidance, authenticity, and spiritual gifts.

Your identity, (truly knowing who you are), your vision, authority, inner guidance (intuition), empowers you to begin to own your place in your life, trusting your actions, and really showing the world what you are truly made of. You empowered your future by planting clear intentions as a natural instinct.

> *"You are ready, qualified in making a huge positive difference in the world."*

These nine chapters create empowering solutions.

INVISIBLE: Embrace the meaning, become and know your own authority, connect with your in-visible self, go in-side and be visible there.

NURTURE: Determination, willing to change, taking steps, beginning to serve and support yourself.

VULNERABILITY: Knowing it is ok to be who you truly are, authentic, brave and bold.

INTENTION: Clarity to what you truly desire. Success comes from focusing intently.

SENSITIVITY: Is such a strength, which helps you with acceptance, and discern your inner truth.

INTUITION: Deep in-side of you there is a place that does know the truth, trust it, let it be your guide.

BELIEVE: The power of believing in yourself and your ability to reaching your goal, must not be under-estimated.

LOVE: Awareness, having the courage to look within. Love is the answer, always choose love over fear.

EMPOWERMENT: Ask yourself those questions, their meaning or judgment, ask if they are empowering or dis-empowering

Powerful times are calling for our higher state of love and empowerment, empowering us to tap into the universal flow of inner love, wisdom and creativity. We are free, let us respond to life with our heart which is ready for receiving and connecting to life.

"I am one with the very power that created me."

Trust in the Divine Plan, continue to strengthen your empowered love. Bless it.

EMPOWERMENT

About the Author

Dawn is a Transformational Healer, Spiritual Teacher and Author. She is a very charismatic soul. Three words that describe her are Passionate, Enthusiastic, and Inspirational. All contributing to the importance of how her life purpose involves communication, whether visible or invisible, to shining her Divine Inner Light that brings Joy and Love to the world.

She is a true Messenger of Love, a powerful leader lovingly guiding others, supporting and encouraging them to connect to who they truly are, helping them feel inspired and uplifted as they pursue their life purpose in their unique and authentic way. Opening their hearts, spreading their love from within as they continue to embrace their

INVISIBLE WINGS.

Contact Dawn:
dawnaurora@hotmail.co.uk
www.spiritofdawn.com

TESTIMONIALS

Dawn's book is simple: "All you need is love."
Step out and take this path to happiness and
enlightenment. Dawn's clear writing, enthusiasm
and supportive voice will help create questions
within yourself, so be prepared for exciting times
ahead. Lots of information and inspirational ideas
to potentially change many lives for the better.

Paul Case
Reiki Master and Healer

Open, authentic, vulnerable
"with brave wings she flies."

Heather Stewart
Celebrant